Paula Matthewson is a political columnist with *The New Daily* and editor of *Despatches*. Her commentary and analysis of Australian federal politics have been published widely since she set aside a long career in politics and advocacy in 2010 to become a freelance writer. During that previous life, Matthewson worked for four years as a Liberal media adviser.

## Writers in the *On Series*

# Paula Matthewson

# On Merit

hachette
AUSTRALIA

*Every attempt has been made to locate the copyright holders for
material quoted in this book. Any person or organisation that may
have been overlooked or misattributed may contact the publisher.*

Published in Australia and New Zealand in 2020
by Hachette Australia
(an imprint of Hachette Australia Pty Limited)
Level 17, 207 Kent Street, Sydney NSW 2000
www.hachette.com.au

First published in 2019 by Melbourne University Publishing

10 9 8 7 6 5 4 3 2 1

Copyright © Paula Matthewson 2019

A catalogue record for this
book is available from the
National Library of Australia

ISBN: 978 0 7336 4419 1 (paperback)

Original cover concept by Nada Backovic Design
Text design by Alice Graphics
Typeset by Typeskill
Author photograph by Kris Baum
Printed and bound in Australia by McPherson's Printing Group

Other than the woman herself, no-one knows for sure why Julie Bishop strode into that press conference wearing those striking red shoes to sign off as Australia's first female foreign minister.

Perhaps Bishop's only intent was to cheer herself up. She'd mentioned in the past that donning a pair of scarlet heels could raise a woman's spirits. And who would begrudge her such a small act of self-comfort if it was what she needed? Just days before, Australia's most popular politician had been very publicly snubbed by colleagues when she ran for the Liberal Party's leadership.

Following Bishop's press conference, Fairfax's award-winning photographer Alex

Ellinghausen posted an unconventional shot of the event on Twitter. The angle was all scarlet heels blazing before the dark masculine suits and shoes of the assembled media. The image flew around the Twittersphere, swiftly symbolising what Bishop's treatment revealed about the Liberal Party: its merit system had been exposed as a sham.

And so, thanks to the keen eye of Ellinghausen and the power of social media, Bishop's red shoes became much more than a potential pick-me-up. They became a rallying point for women who'd had enough—with the Liberal boys' club that used intimidation to subdue them, and the discredited principle of 'merit' to suppress them.

These women became a nascent political movement, one that threatens to overturn decades of Liberal thinking—and rhetoric—that insists Liberal women can only succeed on merit. While they may have once been known for wearing conservative blue, the women of the right have begun to adopt the tactics of those clad in socialist red.

During the weeks that followed Bishop's press conference, her favoured red shoe emoji became the emblem of that emerging resistance. Female Liberal MPs wore touches of red to parliament to repudiate claims by many Liberal men—and traditionalist Liberal women—that their party couldn't possibly have an unconscious gender bias and there was 'nothing to see here'.

Their crimson jackets, dresses and heels—along with a few incendiary statements—signalled the potential beginning of a long-overdue rebellion against the merit myth.

The collective behaviour of these women marked a fundamental shift in the way they viewed the world, as well as themselves. The 'old' way of thinking was steeped in Liberal tradition, based on the values and beliefs that had long been celebrated in the first speeches of (mostly male) Liberal MPs. The importance of individual freedom usually came first in their list of guiding principles, followed by the superiority of market forces and the need for reward to be based on merit. Equality was expressed as the right to equal opportunity but not necessarily to equal outcomes.

Even though they were also committed individualists, these modern Liberal women appeared to have come to the begrudging acceptance that no individual woman, not even one as well-credentialed as Julie Bishop, could overcome the gender bias that flourished within the Liberal Party's male-dominated culture. The flashes of red not only indicated their frustration, rage and disappointment, they also signalled the acceptance by Liberal women that they'd have to follow the lead set by the 'sisterhood' on the other side of politics to achieve equality in their own party. They'd have to use collective action to bring about change.

The importance of this shift can't be over-stated. Collective action doesn't come easily to most Liberals because of their sacrosanct belief in the importance of the individual. This also explains what is for many observers a contradiction among Liberal women: the party has a long history of female parliamentarians fighting to advance the rights of Australian women, but until recently most resisted calling themselves feminists. That's because women on the conservative side of politics equate feminism with activism, public protests and revolutionary change. Collective action. The Liberal way is to work individually within society's structures to create incremental change.

As the party's most senior woman, Bishop had been a prominent defender of those

Liberal principles. She had emphasised the responsibility of individuals to strive for excellence and, if they failed, to accept that failure was due to their own limitations. A year after becoming the first Australian woman to hold the foreign affairs portfolio, Bishop told a women's magazine that she still refused to call herself a feminist and urged women not to use gender as an excuse for being unable to achieve their goals. 'Stop whingeing, get on with it and prove them all wrong' was the advice she proffered.

When asked about this rejection of the feminist label a few weeks later, Bishop doubled down, telling the National Press Club that she didn't deny the existence of the 'glass ceiling' but preferred to ignore it: 'The approach I've taken is that if I want something, I'll work hard and set my mind to it. And if it comes off that's great. If it doesn't, I'm not going to blame the fact that I'm a woman. I'm not going to look at life through the prism of gender.'

True to her word, Bishop hasn't overtly suggested that her tilt for the Liberal leadership failed because she's a woman. Instead, she's directed a lot of attention to the unequal treatment of Liberal women. She used her first speech after resigning as foreign minister, at the *Australian Women's Weekly* Women of the Future awards on 5 September 2018, to highlight the pressing need for a 'broader debate about workplace culture', including 'allegations of bullying, harassment and coercion and the unequal treatment of women'.

As she stood before the media pack that day in late August, resplendent in her crimson heels, Bishop did, however, call out her party for only paying lip service to the principle of merit. When asked whether the Liberal Party would ever elect a popular woman as leader, she pointedly mused, 'Well, when we find one, I'm sure we will.'

If the Liberal Party did select and elect on merit, as it claimed, Bishop should have been a shoo-in to replace Malcolm Turnbull as prime minister. She had the experience and the profile, and the voters loved her. According to the published opinion polls, she entered the leadership contest as the people's choice for Liberal leader, and was more competitive against Labor leader Bill Shorten than Turnbull or any of the other leadership contenders. The twenty-year veteran of federal parliament was also widely acknowledged as whip-smart, articulate, a diligent minister and a formidable fundraiser.

Yet Bishop's eminent suitability for the top job had very little to do with the outcome of the leadership vote. She was eliminated in the first round, leaving the two male candidates—treasurer Scott Morrison and home affairs minister Peter Dutton—to fight it out in the second. It later emerged that some of Bishop's colleagues in the progressive faction (called 'moderates' in the Liberal Party) had abandoned the then foreign minister in a tactical play to get Morrison over the line. Apparently these men had concluded she would lose in a head-to-head contest with their mutual rival, Dutton.

This revelation gives weight to the argument subsequently made by Liberal conservatives that Bishop's loss was due to factional, not gender, issues. It was a reasonable expectation to anticipate that Morrison's supporters in the 'soft' right would shift to the hard right's candidate, Dutton, rather than vote for Bishop if their man was defeated in the first round of voting.

But as chief political writer Annabel Crabb observed in an analysis piece for ABC News on the day of Bishop's iconic press conference, the question wasn't so much whether Bishop was rejected as Liberal leader because she was a woman, but whether a similarly credentialed man would have been treated the same way. Crabb also noted that Liberal men had form when it came to excluding Bishop from decisions that directly affected her, just as her moderate colleagues had done during this most recent leadership spill:

> In 2009, the last time the Liberal Party tied itself up in elaborate knots trying to get rid of Malcolm Turnbull, the height of the leadership machinations saw [the deputy Liberal leader] Ms Bishop attend a crisis meeting in [shadow treasurer] Joe Hockey's office during which a group of her male colleagues sat around discussing who would run for the deputy's role. Mr Hockey suggested that [shadow minister for health and ageing] Peter Dutton would run. Ms Bishop—stunned to

hear her own job being canvassed as if she weren't even present—kept her counsel.

Taken in isolation, it might seem an over-reaction to infer from Bishop's recent experience that the Liberal Party has a gender-bias problem. But the snub didn't occur in a vacuum. It occurred against a backdrop of Liberal women historically being sidelined by men for senior positions in the organisational wing of the party, Cabinet posts in Liberal governments, and safe seats in parliament. The story doesn't get much better in modern times, with women pre-selected for only 18 per cent (that's 7 out of 39) of the party's safe seats at the federal election in 2016.

Added to this is the litany of bad behaviour inflicted upon female federal Coalition

MPs by their male colleagues during the tumultuous days that led up to the leadership vote. For those women, the intimidation and bullying were the latest example of the hyper-masculine culture that had long dominated the Liberal Party—not only within the parlia-mentary wing but also the party organisation. Several of the young, Christian family men whose names were mentioned in relation to the alleged intimidation also happen to be factional heavyweights in their respec-tive state Liberal organisations. And several of the women who subsequently spoke out claimed their preselections were threatened if they didn't support Dutton.

So perhaps it wasn't just the crimson shoes. Perhaps it was also the #MeToo movement that emboldened these women to expose the bullyboy tactics, denouncing the Liberal men who cruelled Bishop's leadership prospects while serving their own. Whatever their reasons, the women ignored suggestions from male colleagues to 'roll with the punches' and went public with their experiences, brandishing the colour red in an unprecedented—and decidedly un-Liberal—expression of solidarity.

It would be an understatement to suggest the red rebellion has been a long time coming. It's been overdue since Tony Abbott unveiled his first ministry after winning government in 2013.

But the Liberal Party's gender imbalance has been simmering as an issue for much longer than that. In 1984, Queenslander Kathy

Martin (later Sullivan) became only the third Liberal woman to be elected to the House of Representatives, forty-one years after Tasmanian Enid Lyons and eighteen years after South Australian Kay Brownbill. Martin shifted to the lower house following ten years in the Senate, where she had been one of four Liberal women. She would remain the sole woman to sit on the Liberals' side of the House for six years.

According to Annemieke Jongsma in *The Biographical Dictionary of the Australian Senate*, Martin was dubbed the 'kissing senator' or 'blonde bombshell' by the media but 'distanced herself from women's liberation activities, maintaining that she was "a Liberal Party candidate and not a women's candidate"'. However, Martin publicly castigated her party after the 1983 federal election, saying the Coalition's loss was attributable to its failure to pay attention to the 'women's vote'. She urged the party to embrace and adapt its policies to the changing dynamics in families and workplaces, and to the changing status of women in society.

Thirty years later, out of the nineteen Liberal and National MPs appointed to the most senior level of the Abbott ministry, the Cabinet, only one woman made the cut. In fact, not even that woman, Julie Bishop, was appointed by Abbott. Thanks to her election as deputy leader by the Liberal party room, she was granted her choice of Cabinet-level portfolio and an automatic seat at the big table.

When Abbott announced the controversial decision on 17 September 2013, he feigned regret that no other Liberal woman had yet attained the level of merit required to be a Cabinet minister. 'Plainly, I am disappointed that there are not at least two women in the Cabinet,' he claimed during the press conference held to announce the new ministry. 'Nevertheless, there are some very good and talented women knocking on the door of the Cabinet.'

Abbott's deference to the so-called merit principle was a slap in the face for the well-credentialed Liberal women he'd chosen to overlook—the worthy women who'd waited patiently to be recognised while a succession of unimpressive men were promoted over them. These men included seat warmers such as two Howard-era former ministers and arch-conservatives, Victorian Kevin Andrews and Tasmanian Eric Abetz, who'd been in parliament for twenty years. Both men also happened to be staunch supporters of Abbott. Then there were non-performers such as Queenslander George Brandis and West Australian David Johnston, who both went straight into Abbott's Cabinet. Meanwhile, the women who are in Cabinet today, the New South Wales moderate Marise Payne, the Victorian moderate Kelly O'Dwyer and the Western Australian right-winger Michaelia Cash, were left to cool their heels in the junior ministries or on the backbench.

The academics and Liberal Party historians Wayne Errington and Peter van Onselen give a fascinating insight into the psychology of that decision in their book *Battleground: Why the Liberal Party Shirtfronted Tony*

*Abbott*. Female Liberal MPs who spoke to Errington and van Onselen for the book suggested that merit had less to do with Abbott's appointments to Cabinet than whether they demonstrated his preferred attributes—aggression and loyalty:

> Most of the women from the parliamentary Liberal Party we spoke to agree that Abbott showed a lack of empathy for women who didn't display masculine attributes—in their debating style, in their aggression, in their drinking and swearing. If Abbott was a man's man, he wanted 'warrior women' around him.
>
> Yet one female MP told us 'Abbott doesn't like women who view the world differently to him and are prepared to express their feelings with conviction.' Warrior

women MPs who he thought did not respect his authority would not prosper under Abbott's leadership.

This tendency is known in the corporate world as mirroring an unconscious bias that leads people to hire in their own image, and it's responsible for creating the gender gap in both business and politics. Instead of putting together a diverse team or, say, a Cabinet that is productive because of its members' complementary skills, the mirroring bias leads to a homogenous team that is weak because its members are yes-men who can't, or won't, question the party line.

One of the Liberal women to put her name to criticism of this phenomenon in the Abbott Government was former Howard Government minister Sharman Stone. While

Stone also served in Abbott's shadow ministry, she was overlooked for a ministerial role in his government. After Abbott lost the leadership and his former chief of staff, Peta Credlin, was reported calling for businesses and governments to do more to address the gender gap, Stone slammed Abbott's ministerial line-up as a backward step for Liberal women, blaming Credlin for not doing more to address the imbalance.

'I think it was a lost opportunity for Peta and if she had perhaps realised the values she's now saying she has, if she'd realised those with Tony, he may have had a better prospect of remaining leader,' Stone told ABC News in September 2015. 'Women felt alienated— they certainly didn't feel part of the team. They certainly looked at our frontbench in the Coalition and saw the row of pale males in suits and didn't feel a part of that.'

However, according to a report in *The Australian* in June 2015 of comments made by Credlin to a Menzies Research Centre forum on gender and politics held that month, the first Abbott Cabinet was practically bare of female ministers because there was a lack of women 'in the pipeline' for senior roles after the 2010 election. 'Our women are not in the safe seats, so when we lose government, we lose our pipeline,' Credlin is reported to have said at the forum. 'So it was really hard to put a ministry together in 2010 when we had just come in touch (with electoral victory)— we didn't have a pipeline of women.'

That was a curious claim to make given there were at least five accomplished and experienced women in the Liberal party room at the time. In addition to Stone there was Payne, who'd been in parliament for sixteen years at the time the Abbott Government was elected; Sussan Ley, the member for Farrer in New South Wales, who'd been an MP for twelve years; Cash, who'd already served five years in the Senate; and O'Dwyer, who'd been in the lower house for four. With the exception of O'Dwyer, all had served in the Coalition's shadow ministry, as had Sophie Mirabella, the member for Indi in Victoria, who would have been the second woman in Abbott's Cabinet if she had not been defeated by the independent Cathy McGowan at the 2013 election.

Malcolm Turnbull recognised the value these women would bring to the government's decision-making processes when he appointed Payne, Ley, Cash and O'Dwyer to Cabinet less than two years later. O'Dwyer joined the small number of Liberal women who'd held treasury portfolios, such as Margaret Guilfoyle (Minister for Finance 1980–83) and Helen Coonan (Minister for Revenue and Assistant Treasurer 2001–04), while Payne became Australia's first female defence minister. Following Bishop's retirement to the backbench, Payne then became Australia's second female foreign minister.

Yet even when confronted with evidence that the Liberal merit principle is little more than a protection racket for men, many Liberal women have remained committed to it. The conservative Cabinet minister and former minister for women, Michaelia Cash, is a typical example, reportedly telling *Crikey* in June 2013 that preselection for women in the Liberal Party 'should recognise merit and excellence rather than be based on some unilateral quota'.

According to the report *Gender and Politics* by the conservative Liberal MP Nicolle Flint and head of the Menzies Research Centre, Nick Cater, quotas are widely rejected in the Liberal Party as 'a top-down, bureaucratic mandate that is anathema to Liberal values and the Liberal conception of democracy'. As a result, Liberal women have been caught in a type of Schrödinger's loop, aware that merit can have nothing to do with the progress of male Liberals, but nevertheless insisting that their own progress be based on it.

The emergence of the red shoe brigade suggests Liberal women may have broken free from this circular thinking. They've begun to acknowledge not only that the Liberals' merit-based system is a sham, but that the claimed reliance on merit will do nothing to increase the number of Liberal women in parliament. There's also a growing awareness that the issue might have an even bigger repercussion than frustrating the careers of talented women: that without increased female representation, the Liberal Party could ultimately drive women voters away. And that means years in the political wilderness.

It's accepted wisdom but a fallacy that the number of Liberal women in federal parliament has steadily declined since Paul Keating's Labor government lost in a landslide to John Howard's Coalition in 1996.

The real story is more nuanced, but no less of an existential threat for Liberal women and, perhaps, their party.

In truth, the total number of female Liberal MPs and senators has remained static since 1996. Twenty-three women featured in the Liberals' parliamentary ranks for most of the eleven years that Howard was in government, dipping to a low of nineteen after Abbott failed to dislodge the Labor government in 2010. That number rose to twenty-one when Abbott finally succeeded in 2013, and rose again to twenty-three following the 2016 federal election.

Even when looking at the proportion of Liberal parliamentarians that are women, the picture isn't much different. Women made up 25 per cent of Liberal MPs during the Howard years, and after dropping at times to 21 per cent, rose back to 24 per cent in 2016 despite Turnbull's disastrous federal election campaign.

So if the number and proportion of Liberal women have barely changed over time, what is it about the Howard win in 1996 that makes people remember it so favourably? Perhaps 1996 is considered a high-water mark due to the record number of Liberal women elected that year. Thirteen female MPs were added to the Liberal Party's ranks in 1996, increasing the total number of Liberal women in federal parliament from eleven to twenty-three. The previous record intake was four new Liberal women elected in 1993 (despite Howard's loss to Keating).

Or perhaps it's because many of the esteemed Liberal women who went on to fight progressive battles within their party were elected in either 1993 or 1996. That honour roll includes the West Australian Judi Moylan, who was part of a Liberal backbench revolt during the Howard years that forced the release of women and children from immigration detention. Victorian Judith Troeth was also part of that group, later crossing the floor to abolish the mandatory billing of asylum seekers for their detention, and support the Rudd Labor government's carbon pollution reduction scheme. And so was Teresa Gambaro, the member for Brisbane, who campaigned during the Abbott years in support of marriage equality.

John Howard may have been the ultimate beneficiary, but he was in no position to take the credit for the wave of female candidates that helped sweep him into office. That feat was due to the efforts of the Liberal Women's Forum, formed in 1993 with the support of then Liberal leader John Hewson to get more Liberal women into parliament. Hewson appointed Dame Margaret Guilfoyle, one of the Liberal Party's original 'women of merit', to chair the forum and champion its work. Guilfoyle had been the first woman to hold a Cabinet-level ministry, in 1975.

Even if the Howard era is sometimes feted as some sort of golden age for Liberal women, closer inspection reveals this to be far from the truth. At first blush, it's impressive that ten of the seventeen women elected for the first time in 1993 or 1996 were appointed to Howard's ministry during his eleven years in office, but only one member of that political generation, Coonan, eventually made it to Cabinet.

That's not to say Howard had a poor record appointing women to Cabinet—he always had at least two female Cabinet ministers, which rose to three and then four in the later years of his government. However, it's difficult to accept that the bounty of accomplished Liberal women elected in 1993 and 1996 did not include at least a few more who were worthy of being appointed to Cabinet over the following decade. If they did exist, Howard chose to squander their potential rather than cultivate it.

Not one of the Liberal women elected for the first time in 1993 or 1996 remains in parliament today, although there are still two serving female parliamentarians who arrived soon after. These are the foreign minister, Payne, who was appointed in 1997 to fill a casual vacancy in the Senate, and her predecessor, Bishop, who was elected in 1998. By contrast, three Liberal men elected in 1993 or 1996 remain: Tony Abbott, Queensland's Warren Entsch, and minister for defence Christopher Pyne. Two other men, Kevin Andrews and Victorian moderate Russell Broadbent, were elected even earlier.

More than half of the Liberal women who were first elected in 1993 or 1996 lost to Labor in subsequent elections, leaving seven members of that cohort to eventually retire on their own terms. By then the Liberal Women's Forum had faded away, allowing Liberal men to regain dominance over the party's preselections. As a result, all but one of those seven women was succeeded by a man.

Moylan's successor was Christian Porter, the former West Australian treasurer. Another Liberal rebel who crossed the floor to support asylum seekers, Danna Vale, was followed in the New South Wales seat of Hughes by Craig Kelly, the staunch Abbott supporter and climate sceptic (although his preselections haven't always been plain sailing). Coonan's place in the senate was filled by New South Wales Liberal Party elder Arthur Sinodinos, who was also the former chief of staff to John Howard. South Australian former journalist Chris Gallus was followed by Simon Birmingham, a long-time Liberal staffer. Birmingham lost that election to Labor, but later became the youngest member of the Senate when he replaced another Liberal woman from the class of 1996, the legendary government whip in the Senate, Jeannie Ferris, after she died from cancer. Gambaro was succeeded by former lobbyist and Liberal staffer Trevor Evans, and Sharman Stone by former president of the National Farmers' Federation Donald McGauchie (although he lost to the Nationals' Damian Drum).

Only the New South Wales MP Joanna Gash was succeeded by a woman—her staffer Ann Sudmalis, who has become a prominent member of the red shoe brigade. A former science teacher and small business operator, Sudmalis was among the women who spoke out after the leadership spill of August 2018 to condemn the culture of intimidation and bullying that pervaded the modern Liberal Party and was particularly directed at women. Due to the bullying she endured, Sudmalis has decided to retire at the next federal election. Of the people who've been suggested in the media to replace her, all are men.

Sudmalis wasn't alone. The former Liberal member for Chisholm in Victoria, Julia Banks, who spectacularly left the party to join the crossbench as an independent in November 2018, also claimed she was 'bullied, pressured and intimidated', in her case by three male colleagues during the lead-up to the leadership spill.

In *Gender and Politics*, Flint and Cater note that out of the fourteen Coalition MPs in predominantly safe seats who've retired since September 2015, thirteen were succeeded by men. Flint was the only new female Liberal MP to succeed a sitting Liberal at the 2016 federal election, while Banks was the only Liberal candidate that year to take a seat off Labor.

With a few notable exceptions, male dominance over Liberal preselections has persisted since the Howard Government was elected in 1996. That dominance hasn't yet significantly affected the number of Liberal women in federal parliament, but it's likely to become an obvious factor if Liberal women in marginal seats lose to Labor candidates in the landslide predicted at the next federal election.

Of the eleven Liberal women currently sitting in the House of Representatives, one has lost preselection to a man, one will retire (and probably be replaced by a man), and another three will likely lose their marginal seats in the expected Labor rout. The potential Liberal candidates being canvassed in the media to replace Banks are all men. Without preselecting additional women to replace them in safe Liberal seats (seats that can withstand a large swing to Labor) or winnable positions on the Senate ticket, the party's female representation in parliament could be reduced at the next election to pre-Howard-era levels.

Even so, there's very little motivation for ambitious men to make way for women with merit when a safe Liberal seat is in the offing. After all, the Liberal Party stands for individual freedom and a competitive market, so it's every man (or woman) for themselves, and may the best man win.

That approach might even work if the Liberal men and women were competing for preselection on a level playing field. But just as there are factors in society that tilt the field towards male players, there are factors in Liberal preselection processes that disadvantage women. One of these factors is that most of the Liberal Party members who sit on preselection panels are white, financially secure boomers. This deeply traditional cohort may mouth the usual platitudes about merit but can be deeply sceptical of a woman's ability to be an effective parliamentarian while she is raising a family.

Such talk overshadowed Kelly O'Dwyer's preselection bid in 2009 for the very safe Liberal seat of Higgins when it was vacated by her former boss, treasurer and deputy Liberal leader Peter Costello. According to the *Sydney Morning Herald* in September 2009, 'some preselectors had reportedly been told that Higgins was "not a seat for a woman because it's a leadership seat", and that questions had been raised about whether Ms O'Dwyer's marriage would last if she won a federal seat'. Of course, O'Dwyer went on to prove the doubters wrong. She became the federal parliament's youngest female Cabinet member and the first serving Cabinet minister to give birth. She also managed to stay married.

However, her detractors didn't give up easily. In April 2017, when O'Dwyer was on maternity leave from Cabinet with her second baby, the *Herald Sun* reported that a posse of disgruntled millionaires had tried to 'conscript' the arch-conservative commentator Peta Credlin to challenge O'Dwyer for preselection. Credlin is the epitome of the 'warrior woman' that van Onselen says Tony Abbott favours, and Abbott has publicly praised her as such on numerous occasions. However, she was politically savvy enough to see that the optics of such a move were all wrong. Writing in *The Australian* at the time, she rejected the claim that she was 'part of a plot by disgruntled locals' to challenge O'Dwyer for preselection as 'complete and utter fake news', noting she had 'always taken a dim view of challenging sitting members'.

This didn't stop the Liberal right-winger from using the opportunity to put the boot into O'Dwyer, who comes from the rival moderate faction.

After posing the question why the young Cabinet minister was vulnerable to challenge in the first place, Credlin alluded to the weakened state of the moderate faction in the Victorian division of the Liberal Party, claiming there were also rumours that O'Dwyer 'no longer has the numbers in her own branches'.

O'Dwyer's example therefore brings us to the other factor that has prevented women of merit from progressing in the Liberal Party: the seemingly never-ending battle between the party's factions. Historically, Liberal women have come from both the right-wing conservative faction and the centre-right moderates. However, the growing dominance of (mostly male) conservatives in the party's state divisions has seen the number of moderate Liberal women (including those from the Class of '96) dwindle over time.

This helps to explain why the Liberal women who were bullied and intimidated during the recent leadership spill included moderates, whose preselections were threatened if they didn't support the conservatives' favoured candidate, Peter Dutton.

Even though they might come from different factions, Liberal women have generally been of one mind when it comes to the question of quotas. Julie Bishop told the ABC's *7.30* on 1 October 2018, 'I think quotas miss the point about merit-based preselections and elections.' Perhaps surprisingly, at least two other members of the red shoe brigade concur.

Victorian senator Jane Hume, whose preselection was threatened during the leadership skirmish, has rejected the idea of quotas.

West Australian senator Linda Reynolds, who took to the Senate to call out the recent bullying behaviour and said she no longer recognised her party, does not identify as a feminist. Like Credlin, Reynolds participated in the forum on gender held by the Menzies Research Centre in June 2015. According to a report in *The Australian* on 29 June of that year, she argued that the Liberal Party had failed to rectify 'the very obvious dissonance' between its unifying and foundation principle of equality of opportunity with its poor record on the equality of opportunity for women. Despite saying this, Reynolds does not support the imposition of quotas.

She told the same forum that quotas were feminists' solution to achieving equality of outcomes, but that this is not an approach I have ever identified with and I believe it does far more harm than good for women today.'

Flint and Cater's report is based in part on the comments made at the forum. They also argue against quotas, claiming that 'while it is tempting to assume that the only way to improve the representation of women in the Liberal Party is to follow the path of Labor, to do so would be to betray the very principles our Party is founded upon'. The two Liberal conservatives strongly reject the imposition of quotas, claiming that 'quotas are part of the semantics of socialist collective action. They are tools preferred in centrally planned command economies. They are anti-democratic and hostile to freedom. They are anathema to Liberalism.'

This resistance stems from the fundamental Liberal belief that success must be achieved through merit rather than special treatment. Following the preselection loss in May 2018 of the Queensland Liberal MP Jane Prentice to a young, male former staffer, the former Liberal senator from Victoria Helen Kroger warned that the Liberals could not afford to go backwards on women. Kroger also noted that she had no problem with quotas, but that the idea of quotas was anathema to most Liberals because it was seen as being 'owned' by Labor.

As some Liberal women have grown to understand that Liberal men without merit are still being rewarded, they've lost their anti-quota fervour and begun to seek other ways to advance. That includes women from the Class of '96, who would likely have worn red in solidarity with Bishop if they were still in parliament today. One of those women would certainly have been Judith Troeth, who originally didn't support quotas but eventually concluded that they were needed to modernise the Liberal Party. 'If the "merit" standard isn't providing greater numbers,' Troeth wrote in September 2015 for *Inside Story* about her June 2010 proposal to introduce quotas for the preselection of women, 'wouldn't logic tell us to try another approach?'

In prosecuting her case over subsequent years, Troeth dispensed with many of the excuses used to resist the adoption of quotas for female Liberal candidates. She argued it was illogical for the party to reject quotas when it already had similar allocations for women in the party organisation. She challenged the myth that only the best candidates would be found by focusing on merit, and that the imposition of quotas meant dropping the bar for achievement levels. And she stressed in 2015 that, given there'd been no significant rise in the number of female Liberal MPs since her earlier proposal, it was time for the party leadership to introduce quotas to boost the number of women.

Troeth took up the cudgels again on 2 December 2018 following the Liberals' disastrous performance in the Victorian state election. Having witnessed the number of Liberal women in the state parliament's lower house drop from six to four, she pressed again for the party to introduce quotas. 'I've certainly seen men of non-merit promoted over women of merit, and the merit argument has been totally discredited in my view,' the former senator for Victoria told ABC News. She then expressed hope that the 'absolutely catastrophic' result in the Victorian election would prompt the Liberal Party to realise it had to not only rebuild from within, but also rebuild trust with the electorate. 'Part of that [process] would be preselecting more women for not only seats in parliament, but safe seats,' Troeth insisted. 'Unless they are in safe seats, they can't possibly hope for career progression and a long time in parliament.'

Sharman Stone, who is now the Australian Ambassador for Women and Girls, was another of that generation's Liberal rebels who argued that quotas for women were needed on the conservative side of politics. In July 2015, she was reported in the *Australian Financial Review* warning of a further contraction in the number of Liberal women if quotas were not set for preselections. Stone said there would be no change in the party's make-up until there were new party regulations and rules, of which quotas for an equal number of male and female candidates at preselections were a starting point. 'You can't sit back and express your sorrow,' she said. 'State by state, we have to agree our preselections will be different, [that] we will require equal numbers in each preselection contest. We will not have a contest until there are women standing there beside the men going for preselection.'

And then there are the Liberal women from more recent generations—such as Sussan Ley, the second woman to join Tony Abbott's Cabinet—who are reconsidering their earlier position because of the failure of things to change. In early September, not long after the latest leadership spill exposed the Liberal Party's toxic culture and poor relationship with women, Ley told ABC Radio National that she wasn't a fan of quotas, 'but I must say recently I've wondered whether we should consider them'. In a follow-up interview with *Guardian Australia* a couple of days later, Ley said it was time for women in the Liberal Party to step up. 'I think the time is right for another look at quotas,' she said, noting that the junior Coalition partner, the Nationals, received a quota of seats in the Cabinet and broader ministry. 'So why can't we find a way of doing this with gender?'

Before eventually leaving the Liberal Party for the crossbench, Julia Banks initially flagged her intention to leave parliament in a statement on 29 August 2018 that denounced the 'scourge of cultural and gender bias, bullying and intimidation [that] continues against women in politics, [in] the media and across business'. In a subsequent late-night speech to parliament on 12 September, Banks said 'the [Liberals'] meritocracy argument is completely and utterly flawed' and that given women represent half the population, 'so should a modern Liberal Party'. Banks also argued that quotas would work as a reset mechanism that could make parliament more representative.

This modest but growing acceptance among Liberal women that quotas may be needed to address their party's gender imbalance appears to be reflected in the views of Liberal supporters. Back in 2013, an Essential poll found that only 17 per cent of Liberal voters were concerned about there being just one woman in the first Abbott Cabinet. However, an Essential poll held one month after the leadership change that brought on the resignation of Julie Bishop in 2018 found a staggering 68 per cent of Liberal voters supported the party adopting quotas to increase the number of Liberal women in the parliament.

Perhaps the best argument in favour of quotas for women in politics is the numbers.

The international Gender Quotas Database currently lists over 130 countries that use gender quotas to overcome 'institutionalised bias against women in politics', as Australian National University academic Marian Sawer described the problem in *The Conversation* in July 2015. 'Thanks to quotas, the proportion of women in parliaments across the world has nearly doubled in the past 20 years.'

During a public lecture on women in leadership at the University of Adelaide on 4 September 2018, former prime minister Julia Gillard noted that 'in 1994 the ALP and the Liberal Party had around about the same percentage of women in their federal caucuses'. This was 14.5 per cent for Labor and 13.9 per cent for the Liberals. 'Today, women are 46 per cent of federal Labor, a jump of over thirty percentage points. In contrast, the Liberal Party has inched forward to 23 per cent, a jump of just over nine percentage points.' Put another way, thirty-seven Liberal women have been elected to the House of Representatives since 1943, and twenty-nine to the Senate. In contrast, sixty-nine Labor women have been elected to the lower house, along with forty to the Senate.

Labor didn't reach these milestones because the party's ambitious men were happy to make way for its talented women. Perhaps the most memorable demonstration of this reality is the 2012 preselection of South Australian factional heavyweight and 'faceless man' Don Farrell, who was awarded the first spot on Labor's Senate ticket, relegating the then finance minister, Penny Wong, to second place. While this was still a winnable position for Wong, it nevertheless created a very bad look for the progressive party. Farrell ended up yielding to pressure from the party's leadership and gave up the top spot to Wong.

To put it bluntly, quotas recognise that men in male-dominated organisations, if left to their own devices, will tend to choose other men. That is, they'll recruit in their own image.

As the political scientists Anika Gauja (University of Sydney), Fiona Buckley (University College Cork) and Jennifer Curtin (University of Auckland) wrote in *The Conversation* in May 2018 following the preselection loss of Jane Prentice, 'the reality is candidate selection is often determined by interpersonal links … Given the male dominance of politics, this practice privileges men, who disproportionately hold positions of power within political parties and tend to recruit and select other men for political office.'

The Labor Party is less wedded than the Liberals are to individual freedoms and will accept restrictions on those rights, such as the imposition of quotas, if the restrictions are for the greater good. Also in *The Conversation*, but after the most recent leadership spill, former journalist and now academic Chris Wallace wrote in September 2018 that 'practical politics runs on quotas. They are the tools of last resort when dominant powers refuse to share power fairly … They work.'

Labor first adopted quotas for women candidates in 1994, committing to preselect women for 35 per cent of winnable seats by

2002. According to Wallace, Susan Ryan, the former Labor minister who was influential in her party's creation of laws to establish equal opportunity for women, wrote in her 1999 biography that Labor's quota rules were 'bitterly resented by many men in the Party, and when they favour a woman from the wrong faction, they upset some women as well'. With the support of the National Labor Women's Network and the activist group EMILY's List Australia, the party's preselection of women increased from 14.5 per cent in 1994 to 35.6 per in 2010. EMILY's List was established in 1999 by a group of Labor women to create the cultural change needed within the ALP to ensure there were sufficient opportunities for women to become candidates and MPs.

Labor currently has a quota of 40 per cent for female MPs, with the goal of reaching 50 per cent by 2025.

While this is clearly good for aspiring female Labor politicians, it's also a vote-winner for the party. One of the main drivers for Labor's adoption of quotas for women in 1994 was the recognition it needed more female candidates and MPs if it was to attract a greater share of the female vote.

According to political scientist Ian McAllister, who conducts the long-running Australian Election Study at the Australian National University, women were 9 per cent less likely to vote Labor than men in 1967, but by 1990 this gap had declined to two percentage points; it jumped back up to six percentage points in 1993. The spike in the number of women turning away from Labor was attributed to the relative unpopularity of Paul Keating, the prime minister at the time. Given Keating's rock-star status with many Labor supporters today, it might be surprising to know that 26 per cent of women in 1993 rated the pugnacious PM at zero on a zero-to-ten scale of popularity. Labor moved to address this 'woman problem' just a year later.

After Keating retired from politics in 1998, the gender gap closed and there was no discernible difference between the way women or men voted for Labor. But then, in 2001, it began to grow in the opposite direction, with women becoming more inclined to vote Labor than men. By 2010 they were

7 per cent more likely than men to do so. This was considered to be due to the popularity of then prime minister Julia Gillard, who rated an average of 5.3 on the same popularity scale. Yet even after Gillard bowed out of politics, the Australian Election Study found that 7 per cent of women were more likely in 2016 to support Labor.

This suggests the Liberal Party is facing the same threat to its survival that confronted Labor in 1993. The only unknown is whether it is willing to adopt a similar strategy—namely, quotas—to ensure its survival rather than stick with 'aspirational targets and mentoring'.

While not a fan of quotas, red shoe brigade member Linda Reynolds has pointed to the UK Conservatives as a possible model for getting more Liberal women into federal parliament: the Tories increased their female representation from 17 to 67 in a decade without quotas by raising awareness of the issue and changing preselection processes. Reynolds' other point about the Conservative Party's experience is that it has run the numbers and determined that it can't win office if its female vote falls below 40 per cent.

Even though Flint and Cater vigorously oppose quotas for Liberal women, they acknowledge a clear understanding of the 'compelling' reason why the party 'must act now to address the underrepresentation of women in its parliamentary ranks'. Drawing on analysis of recent elections that suggest 'parties with a better balance of men and women have greater electoral appeal', the pair note that the Liberals' support among women relative to men has waned since 2001 and that 'the strengthening of Labor's female vote has coincided with a noticeable increase in the number of Labor women pre-selected in winnable seats'.

Another Liberal woman in red, Jane Hume, pointed this out in response to the 2018 Victorian state election rout. In an opinion piece for the *Australian Financial Review* in November 2018, the Victorian senator warned:

> The lesson learnt here is that we must know and understand the issues that matter before we focus on them ... It's hard to understand an electorate if you don't reflect it. Female representation in the Liberal Party is no longer an issue of aesthetics but

an electoral imperative. The rise of centre-right female independents in previously Liberal-held safe seats cannot be ignored. The leaders that champion and facilitate the introduction of significantly more women to our parliamentary team—in safe seats that allow them time to rise through the ranks—will leave a legacy as important as the traditional Liberal heroes.

It could be argued that the Liberal Party is now facing an even greater threat than Labor did in 1993, due to the number of talented centre-right women either sitting on the cross-bench or considering a run for parliament as independents at the next election—perhaps even against such high-profile conservative

men as Tony Abbott and former deputy prime
minister Barnaby Joyce.

Fiona Simson, the chair of peak lobby
group the National Farmers' Federation, is
the latest high-profile woman to be associated
with talk of a wave of independent female
candidates running in safe Liberal and
National seats in 2019. This 'other' unofficial
women's movement was distinct from the
Liberals' red rebellion until Banks decamped
to the crossbench in late 2018. Now the two
forces have the potential to merge, creating
a perfect storm for change that is driven by
women to advance women.

The first inkling of an independent wom-
en's 'movement' began at the 2013 federal
election when country independent Cathy

McGowan snatched the Victorian seat of Indi from the Liberal MP Sophie Mirabella. Indi had been held since 1931 by one or another of the conservative parties. It was a close result, with McGowan prevailing by 431 votes thanks to strong preference flows from Labor and the Greens. She won again in 2016, increasing her margin to 4.6 per cent of the vote.

That election also saw Rebekha Sharkie take the blue-ribbon South Australian seat of Mayo from the Liberals. Sharkie is a member of the Nick Xenophon Team (NXT) and not technically an independent, but with the renaming of NXT to Centre Alliance and the withdrawal of Xenophon from political life, she is increasingly perceived to be operating as one. When Sharkie defeated her former boss, the disgraced Liberal MP Jamie Briggs, with the help of Labor preferences in 2016, she became the first woman and non-Liberal ever to hold the seat. She had to compete for it again in 2018 after resigning over dual-citizenship problems. Initially written off, she not only won the seat but increased her primary vote by nearly 10 per cent.

Kerryn Phelps is the latest flag-bearer for the female independents, obliterating the Liberal Party's long-term hold on Wentworth following the resignation of former PM Malcolm Turnbull. Reflecting the success of independents in Indi and Mayo, Phelps' election could be attributed to three major factors.

First, she was a high-profile woman with a centrist philosophy and an agenda that appealed to a broad range of voters who were disgruntled, frustrated or unhappy with the status quo. Second, her skilled team ran a formidable grassroots campaign. And third, Phelps was able to get over the line due to Labor and the Greens running complementary campaigns. Both parties directed their preferences to her, and Labor ran dead to ensure she was in the best position (second place) to benefit from those preferences.

A similar three-pronged strategy could deliver in 2019 what the Liberal and National parties have seemingly been incapable of achieving this century: the election of high-quality female candidates in safe Coalition seats around the country. But instead of sitting on the Coalition benches, these women will sit on the crossbench, holding the balance of power. Simson could be one of those 'women of merit' if she decides to run against Joyce in New England.

It's no coincidence that this movement of independent candidates responding to voter unhappiness with the status quo is made up of women. It's also no coincidence that these women sense the emergence of a voter uprising in traditional Coalition electorates. In addition to the Liberal women wearing red, female voters are fed up with the hyper-masculine and strictly conservative ethos that continues to pervade the Liberal and National parties and is perpetuated in the selection of candidates for most safe seats. According to the Australian Election Study, 47 per cent of men voted for the Coalition at the 2016 federal election, but only 38 per cent of women did so. Given the choice to vote for high-quality centrist candidates who also happen to be women, there's a high probability that many of those female voters will choose the alternative at the 2019 election and abandon the Coalition.

Such a shift has been foreshadowed in the opinion polls. In late September 2018, the Essential poll was tracking the Coalition's vote from women at 33 per cent and Labor's at 37 per cent, although Peter Lewis, the head of Essential Media warned in his *Guardian Australia* column on 25 September: 'The big gender gap in the Liberal vote could be a symptom or cause of its current malaise. Are more men supporting the Liberals because they are a party of middle-aged blokes, or is the control of middle-aged blokes just making the party less attractive to women?'

It's difficult to tell whether Julie Bishop's rebuff marks a new low in the prospects of worthy Liberal women or is simply a signpost on their descent to oblivion. Is this as low as it gets, or is it a taste of even worse things to come? That could depend on how organised these fiercely independent women are prepared to get.

The Liberal Party has a target of increasing the proportion of its female federal MPs to 50 per cent by 2025, but has no strategy to reach that target.

The more conservative-minded Liberals who remain committed to the merit myth believe the best way to achieve gender equity in their party is essentially to do more of the same: identify, mentor and shepherd women of merit. Unsurprisingly, this is the almost universal view among the Liberal men who are prepared to concede the party's gender imbalance is an authentic problem.

Even when admitting there are obstacles to the progression of Liberal women, Prime Minister Scott Morrison argued that he'd never supported quotas and didn't believe they were the way 'you remove obstacles'. And he doesn't shy away from using the M-word. In an interview with ABC's *7.30* in September 2018, Morrison explained 'I believe in any political organisation [progression] should be a matter of one's own credibility, exertion, work and merit.'

Bishop's replacement as deputy Liberal leader, Victoria's Josh Frydenberg, similarly insisted during an interview with the ABC's *Insiders* program the same month that 'we're all focused on improving those numbers' of Liberal women using 'recruitment, retention, [and] mentoring, which is absolutely critical here in order to get more women into these seats'.

The Liberals' chief traditionalist, former prime minister John Howard, weighed into the debate while launching his latest book at the Tattersall's Club in Brisbane, which doesn't allow women to become members. Howard said he'd like to see more Liberal women in the House of Representatives, but the whole notion of quotas was wrong and patronising: 'In the end, you've always got to make a judgement based on merit.' There's that word again.

The Liberals' highest-profile moderate, Christopher Pyne, said in an interview with

*7.30* in July 2015 that the Liberals had 'suffered in the last decade or so in not having enough women in our party room' but that people should be elected on merit, not targets or quotas. However, he also conceded that 'if merit isn't achieving the outcome that you want, then other measures need to be looked at to ensure that we are attracting women to parliament'. The politician, who claims to be a 'fixer', doesn't appear to have a plan for fixing this particular problem.

Meantime, the progressive New South Wales Liberal MP Craig Laundy took a few tentative steps to being the first man in the party to support quotas for women. He told *The Australian* on 11 September 2018 that while he agreed completely 'with the principle of merit-based preselections', where we find [ourselves] today is at a disproportionate representation of men versus women'. Laundy reportedly said the Liberals wouldn't be able to adequately increase female representation from where it was without using quotas. 'We need to change this and perhaps a first step is short-term intervention with a quota system in safe seats and selected safe Senate spots so the party can grow its female representation to the 50/50 level.' It's notable that Laundy was also one of the few Liberal men to remain in the chamber when Banks delivered her bombshell resignation speech to Parliament in November.

Somewhat surprisingly, Laundy's conservative colleagues in the Victorian Liberal Party appear to agree. According to a report in Fairfax Media in December 2018, the

Victorian 'conservative powerbroker' Marcus Bastiaan 'pushed for quotas to be considered' at a party meeting held just days before, in response to the Victorian state election.

An approach based on 'merit' has clearly failed to increase the number of Liberal women in parliament. It's also failed to fend off an impending decline in numbers that could soon render Liberal women a threatened species. As Judith Troeth said in 2010 and more recently, it's time to try another approach.

The red rebellion has already demonstrated that part of that approach involves a necessary calling-out of the toxic culture that pervades both the parliamentary and organisational wings of the Liberal Party. As Gauja, Buckley and Curtin so aptly put it in

*The Conversation*, 'the interaction of right-wing values with masculine institutions is not particularly empowering of, or for, women'. Only by making it crystal clear that the status quo is unacceptable will the rebels have any chance of persuading the party's more traditional women (and men) of the need to take drastic action, such as adopting quotas.

One of the Liberal women who exposed the bullying, South Australian senator Lucy Gichuhi, stated that the party had a problem with women. Fairfax Media reported on 27 November that Gichuhi stressed: 'That is a fact. It's open for anybody to see … So if we can start by accepting we have a problem, we address it … and stop beating up our women, that's all we have to do.'

Is it that simple?

The resistance will be strong and probably intemperate, and will most likely involve the gaslighting of women who demand change. They'll be undermined with accusations of seeing bias where it doesn't exist, or of over-reacting. There may even be obtuse references to their emotionally vulnerable state. We know this because that's what happened to the Liberal women who called out bullying and gender bias during and after the 2018 leadership stoush. Liberal men, including the prime minister, and even some Liberal women denied the bullying had occurred and insisted there was 'nothing to see here'. Others implied the women were being 'princesses' and needed to toughen up.

For example, another of the party's warrior women, Liberal vice-president Teena

McQueen, used her appearance as a panellist on Sky News on 17 September to challenge the women who exposed the bullying to 'put up or shut up', adding that 'women always want the spoils of victory without the fight'. Another female apologist for the Liberal boys' club, Credlin, was equally scathing, particularly of 'the deserter' Banks after she moved to the crossbench. In her *Sunday Telegraph* column on 2 December, Credlin accused Banks of 'spectacularly dumping on the party that put her into parliament', and described her resignation speech as not only self-serving, self-important and self-deluded, but also a 'betrayal of the real Liberals who worked hard to win the election in her seat'.

Credlin also claimed that Banks wouldn't run in Chisholm again because 'it is too much hard work', and that her move to the cross-bench 'was presumably a chess play to set up a post-political career as professional victim'. 'Otherwise, if genuine,' Credlin concluded, Banks 'would have raised concerns about the treatment of women long ago when she had the ear of the former PM and could do something about it. And there would be specific allegations; yet three months after her sweeping claims, there's still nothing.'

Turnbull, aided by MPs who 'trad[ed] their vote for a leadership change in exchange for their individual promotion, pre-selection endorsements or silence. Their actions were undeniably for themselves, for their position in the party, their power, their personal ambition, not for the Australian people who we represent.'

Banks then argued that:

equal representation of men and women in this Parliament is an urgent imperative which will create a culture change. There's the blinkered rejection of quotas and support of the merit myth. But this is more than a numbers game. Across both major parties, the level of regard and respect for women in politics is years behind the business world. There is also a clear need for an independent whistleblower system as found in many workplaces to enable reporting of misconduct of those in power without fear of reprisal or retribution.

To those who say politics is not for the faint hearted and that women have to toughen up, I say this: the hallmark

characteristics of the Australian woman,
and I've met thousands of them, be they in
my local community, in politics, business,
the media, or sport, are resilience and a
strong, authentic, independent spirit.

The speech was dismissed by Liberal men in
coded language as little more than the actions
of an emotionally fragile woman. Fairfax
Media reported in November that, following
her initial speech in September on bullying, Banks had been subject to a whispering
campaign that attempted to intimidate her
into silence. In public, Liberals hinted that
Banks could not stand the heat of the political kitchen. In private, they claimed she was a
'difficult' woman who had needed enormous
help to win her seat at the 2016 election.

Banks may have seen this coming. In her earliest statement, on 29 August, she warned those who would accuse her of playing the gender card that she would continue to fight for gender equality because 'women have been silent for too long'.

Banks was initially persuaded to stay on until the 2019 election to avoid throwing the Morrison Government into minority status. However, that happened anyway when Phelps was elected in Turnbull's old seat of Wentworth. Following further undermining and gaslighting by her Liberal 'colleagues', Banks decamped to the crossbench, adding one more to the growing number of female independents in the parliament.

In its November story, Fairfax Media reported that Banks had endured a 'series of claims by anonymous Liberals who tried to blacken her name'. Banks called out that intimidation and gaslighting during her resignation speech: 'Often, when good women call out or are subject to bad behaviour, the reprisals, backlash and commentary portray them as the bad ones—the liar, the troublemaker, the emotionally unstable or weak, or someone who should be silenced.'

As Marian Sawer put it in her July 2015 piece for *The Conversation*, 'Those campaigning for gender equity in Australian politics need a great deal of stamina. Those pushing for quotas in the Liberal Party may have this stamina, but they are from the wrong faction and are up against entrenched resistance. It's unlikely that the partisan gender gap will be closed any time soon.'

It's one thing for the women who've lost preselection, decided to retire at the next election or left the Liberal Party altogether to agitate for the party to confront its 'woman problem'. It will be the women who agitate for change from positions of power within the party who have the best chance of driving the necessary reforms.

Kelly O'Dwyer, an avowed feminist, is showing the way. She told *7.30* in September 2018, following the reports of bullying, that she was 'a little bit disgusted' by the treatment of these women and the implications that they were being snowflakes or princesses. O'Dwyer was also reported in the *Herald Sun* in November telling the prime minister in a crisis meeting after the Victorian election that their party was now seen as a group of 'homophobic, anti-women, climate-change deniers'. This was in response to the party being abandoned by its supporters in the state election, even in previously safe Liberal seats.

The other openly feminist Liberal Cabinet minister, Marise Payne, told ABC Radio in September 2018 that the party had a 'very serious' problem with the number of women in parliament. 'I think that we do have a very serious issue concerning the role of women in the parliamentary process and also in efforts to engage more across the community,' the foreign affairs minister said. 'We did a very good job in 1996 … to ensure we had a very broadly representative team facing the community. We've proven we can do it, I know that we can do it again, and we have to bring the same determination as we brought those many years ago to addressing this task now.'

Speaking on the ABC's *RN Drive* on the same day, former Liberal Cabinet minister Ley said of her recent conversion to the potential value of quotas, 'If you look at our party, the picture tells its own story.' Linda Reynolds had been agitating for change even before Prentice was dropped in May 2018, and was reported by ABC News in November 2017 saying that she and her female colleagues had a personal responsibility to drive cultural change through the party and get more women into parliament. 'Women make amazing MPs and local representatives,' Reynolds said, 'but sometimes they just need to see other women and hear from other women and see that it is possible.'

Also in response to Prentice, O'Dwyer created the Enid Lyons Fighting Fund to make sure Liberal women have financial support for their campaigns. Lyons was not only the first Liberal woman to be elected to federal parliament, but the first woman altogether. She was also the first to be appointed to Cabinet, although she wasn't given a ministerial portfolio. As Jacqueline Maley pointed out in May 2018 in a Fairfax Media article about O'Dwyer's new fighting fund, 'there are other parts of the Lyons story [that] are not boasted so proudly' by Liberals: 'Like her disappointment at not being offered a portfolio. Or her complaint that her vice-presidency [of the Executive Council] was a "toothless position", or her remark that her colleagues "only wanted me to pour the tea".'

As the minister for women, O'Dwyer runs networking sessions in Parliament House for female Liberal MPs, and reportedly has plans to establish a training course on leadership for women that will be available to all political staff. She has also rolled out or announced a suite of policies designed— at least in part—to re-establish the Liberal Party's relevance to women. These will be contested and debated within the highly charged and partisan political environment that is Australian politics today. Given that the relative merits of the policies are likely to be dissected and dismissed, they may be less powerful in attracting the female vote to the Liberals than hoped.

Labor's experience (along with that of the female independents) appears to powerfully demonstrate that the most effective way to win the support of women voters is to have high-quality, engaging and authentic women candidates. The challenge for the Liberals is to find the best way to achieve this. As Bishop noted, there is a lot to be done. The party has started to make an effort by preselecting women for the first position on its Senate ticket in several states—or at least the second position, which is still winnable even if Labor is returned in a landslide.

But increasing the number of Liberal women in the Senate will only go halfway to closing the gender gap. The Liberals must put female candidates in safe seats—using quotas or some other way that resists men appointing other men—if the party is to have any chance of meeting its 50 per cent 'target' by 2025.

If nothing is done to address the imbalance, the party is likely to have an outcome similar to 2016, when the Liberals fielded women in only 18 per cent (that is, 7) of its 39 safe seats. Meantime, Labor preselected women for 35 per cent (16) of its 46 safe seats.

Julie Bishop may never tell us why she wore those scarlet shoes to address the media that day, but she's left us in no doubt about her views on the Liberal Party's poor treatment of women. The most accomplished Liberal woman in federal parliament appears to have dropped the old assurances about merit now they've been proven to be empty. Instead, she's taken to denouncing the bad behaviour of the Liberal boys' club and encouraging Liberal women to actively campaign for equality rather than wait passively for it to happen.

A week after the leadership spill, Bishop used her high-profile speech at the *Australian Women's Weekly* Women of the Future awards to challenge the Liberal Party to do more than pay lip service to advancing equality for women. She said it was untenable for women to make up less than 25 per cent of Liberal MPs in 2018, and that it was high time the party recognised it had a problem in attracting and maintaining diversity. 'It is not acceptable for our party to contribute to the fall in Australia's ratings from fifteenth in the world in terms of female representation in 1999, to fiftieth today,' she said.

Bishop also used the speech to denounce the bullying behaviour that had been exposed during the leadership spill, confessing that she had witnessed behaviour in Canberra that 'wouldn't be tolerated in any other workplace'. 'Unacceptable workplace practices are the responsibility of us all—to identify it, to stop it, to fix it … We are adults. We are grown people. We have to take responsibility for our own personal behaviour,' Bishop stressed that day. 'When a feisty, amazing woman like Julia Banks says "this environment is not for me", don't say "Toughen up, princess"—say "Enough is enough".'

Following Banks' resignation from the Liberal Party and shift to the lower-house crossbench, Bishop said the move 'saddened' her because Banks would be missed, and her departure highlighted the party's need for more 'strong, centrist women'. Speaking at an Ernst & Young conference in November, Bishop argued that 'No party can meet its potential without ensuring it has an equal number of women in its ranks ... Fifty per cent of our population is female, 51 per cent in Australia, and that applies to the Liberal Party as well as the rest of the country.'

Judging by the number of Liberal women who've responded to Bishop's call for action, brandishing their own flourishes of red and sharing messages of resistance, a new Liberal women's 'movement' appears to have emerged. In contrast to the short-lived Liberal Women's Forum of the 1990s, this movement may last longer and have more impact by drawing strength from the Liberal women who appear ready to use collective action to drive change, and may even have an open mind about the use of quotas.

During an interview with Fairfax Media on 27 November, Bishop described her role in this movement as a 'lightning rod for discussion about women in politics'. She said women had approached her in shops, in airports and on the street to talk about the leadership vote. Some were angry on her behalf, and some were disheartened. But Bishop said she makes an effort to respond to them with a positive and uplifting message: 'My advice is to back yourself, back your judgement and your intuition, set your own high standards and don't be distracted by those who criticise you for not reaching their standards and couldn't or wouldn't reach those standards themselves.'

Having initiated the red rebellion, Bishop's greatest challenge will be to maintain its momentum. Perhaps this is what she had in mind when she recently donated her red satin block-heeled pumps to the Museum of Australian Democracy. According to the museum, 'the shoes were seen as a bold statement and a symbol of solidarity and empowerment among Australian women'.

During the official ceremony to hand over the shoes and in numerous associated media interviews, Bishop remarked that she had no idea the impact of wearing them to the press conference would have, and was surprised 'so many people read so much' into the shoes. 'Red is one of my favourite colours,' she explained in the Fairfax Media interview. 'It evokes power, passion and fashion. In power

I always noted that many nations have red in their flags and that's because it symbol- ises courage and freedom. Passion, well, you know—red hearts, red roses. And fashion, that's why they call it a red carpet—and red lipstick, red nail polish, red shoes … Since that time, many people have told me the col- our red should be a symbol of solidarity and empowerment among Australian women. The red shoe emoji has taken on a life of its own.'

Now those crimson shoes will be a per- manent reminder of the avowed blue-blood Liberal woman who put her foot down for gender equality.